5-Minute NATURE STORIES

WRITTEN BY
Gabby Dawnay

ILLUSTRATED BY
Mona K

MAGIC CAT PUBLISHING

NEW YORK

In this book, you'll find 5-minute nature stories to read aloud.

Each one is an everyday miracle . . . waiting to be discovered by you!

At the end of each story, explore an informative "ALL ABOUT" page with a grown-up.

All about BEES and POLLINATION

POLLINATION is the journey that flowering plants take to reproduce. It happens when pollen is moved from one flower to another and it allows the plant to make seeds that will grow into new plants. Many plants rely on POLLINATORS to move the pollen from flower to flower. Bees are pollinators, so they are an essential part of this process.

1. A flower's male parts make a powdery substance called POLLEN.

2. A bee picks up the powdery pollen as it flies from flower to flower!

3. POLLINATION happens when the bee drops pollen on another flower. The flower will go on to make seeds.

7. The honeybee WAGGLE DANCE is a figure-of-eight boogie that tells other bees the exact location of a food supply. (It's basically bee sat nav!)

All sorts of plants rely on bees to pollinate them, and bees need plants to live and make honey. A third of our food is thanks to bees. We simply can't exist without them!

6. As a reward for the bees' hard work, flowers give them a sugary liquid called NECTAR. And it's nectar that bees make into their most famous product: glorious, golden honey!

5. Bees carry the pollen they collect in mini-saddlebags on their legs.

4. The bees also gather the pollen to take back to feed their family.

82

Which **5-minute NATURE STORY** will you read today?

The MYSTERY of MUSHROOMS

Under the leaves,
by the roots of the trees,
an explosion of spores
flickers up in the breeze.

With a huff from the wind
and a puff from the ground,
like a sprinkle of wishes,
they flutter around.

"*Yay!*" cry the little spores. "*We're on our way!*"
as they scatter about
in a blossoming spray.

Floating and dipping, they drift to and fro,
getting carried along by the wind's ebb and flow.

Farther and farther
they criss and they cross,
until some come to land
on a patch made of moss.

"Here we will rest!" And the spores make a bed,
where they'll start to produce an unraveling thread!

And soon . . .

Snug in the mud
of an underground space,
a mycelium spreads
in a pattern like lace.

Blooming through mold
both earthy and lush,
is a tangle of tendrils
in the underground hush.

Connecting and growing,
it moves with the flow
of the forest above
and the forest below.

It eats and digests
all the rot of the wood
like a super-converter
of yuck into good!

Oh, marvelous fungus—
what networking skill!
It will grow and connect
with its neighbors until . . .

The next stage emerges:
a button so cute,
pushing out of the earth
as a shiny new fruit!

With a sprinkle
of rain
and a dabble
of dew . . .

"Why hello, Mushroom One!
And hello, Mushroom Two!"

A cluster of mushrooms
emerge in a group!
(Did you know when they spread,
you can call them a "troop"?)

Mushroom One,
Mushroom Two,
Mushroom Three,
Mushroom Four—
mushrooms all over
the mossy-green floor!

For wherever there's one,
there are more to be found,
every one sending spores
till they grow all around!

Oh, the mystery of mushrooms
that grow underground.
It's a wonderful miracle
merry-go-round!

All about MUSHROOMS

Mushrooms are not plants or animals, but belong to a special group-or kingdom-of their own called FUNGI.

1. The MUSHROOM head fans out, forming a fruiting body and releasing SPORES.

2. The SPORES grow into HYPHAE.

3. The HYPHAE form KNOTS.

MUSHROOMS grow from tiny spores-and when spores land, they grow into tiny white fibers called HYPHAE. These hyphae spread out into an underground network of threads called a MYCELIUM that live, grow, and feed the mushroom. They help decompose and eat plant waste, making the soil richer. When the time is right, the hyphae form KNOTS. These push through the soil into tiny buttons . . . which turn into mushrooms!

5. The mushroom matures.

4. A button appears-the head of a BABY MUSHROOM!

Now look at the **SPORES**
drifting up through the air.

But where are they going?
Let's follow them there . . .

The WOOD WIDE WEB

Can you imagine—
amazing, but true,
that the trees of the wood
have an internet too?

Trees are not lonely.
They live in groups
and they stretch out their roots
to connect in a loop.

The branches above have a network below
that gathers the nutrients needed to grow.

Each tentacle "talks" in an interlinked flow.
Oh, the web of the wood is connected . . . like so!

But the chatter of trees
doesn't make any sound,
for their secrets are spread
through the roots underground.

Gazillions of microbes
discuss this and that
on whispering channels
of underground chat.

How does this happen?
Let me explain.
Fungi work with the trees
like a super-cool brain!

Encircling roots in a gentle embrace,
these fabulous fungi are all over the place.

The wonderful webbing majestically spreads
all the messages on a network of threads . . .

"*There's food for you here,*"
says one tree to another,
while seedlings are fed
in the shade of their mother.

Without any sunlight,
it's tricky to feed,
so the mother tree's roots
give them all that they need!

"Help!" cries the sapling,
"These aphids are sticky!"
And other trees know
that the problem is tricky.

"We need aphid-eaters!"
They send out a call,
because working together
is better for all.

The trees gain their strength
from the fungi below,
which give them the nutrients
needed to grow.

They breathe when it's light
and they feed when it's dark.
Their leaves toughen up
and they harden their bark.

And trees give the fungi
a sugary treat,
making the partnership
fully complete!

A friendship with fungi
will keep them alive
so the web of the wood
can continue to thrive.

All about the WOOD WIDE WEB

The wood wide web is the way all forests are connected underground: a communication network that stretches for miles and miles right under our feet! A fine web of fungi grows around and into the roots of trees. This gives nutrients (food) to the trees. In return, the trees give the fungi sugars and a place to reproduce. This happy partnership is called MUTUALISM.

The WOOD WIDE WEB enables trees to talk to one another.

As forests communicate, cooperate, and swap information like one giant brain, some scientists say they should be thought of as a single SUPER-ORGANISM!

If a tree is under attack from tiny, sticky aphid bugs, it sends out chemical signals through its roots to warn neighboring trees.

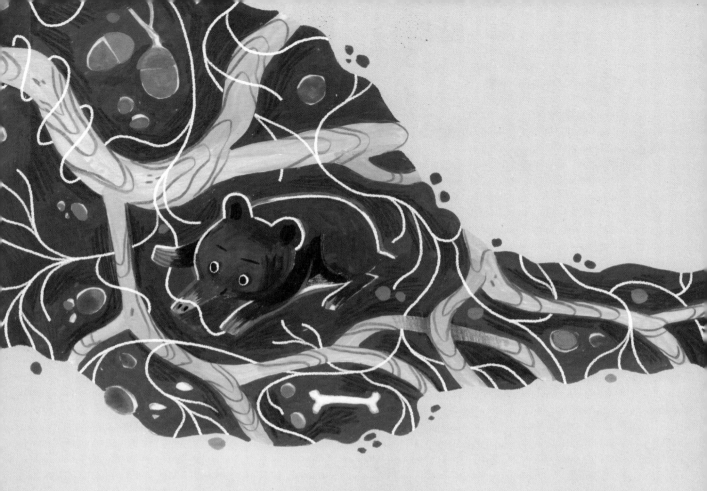

An invisible **WEB**
that connects every tree.

But where will it lead us?
Let's follow and see . . .

The SONG of the DEER

Out of the velvety,
vanishing night,
a fairy-tale animal
strolls into sight.

It turns with a look
and then moves on its way,
from the gray of the dawn
to the break of the day.

Another appears—
like a ghost in the mist,
or a whispering shadow
that might not exist.

A fawn and her mother approach side-by-side,

and they all stop and drink where the river runs wide.

Watching with eyes
that are ebony black,
together they turn
and return to the track.

They amble and graze
on the glittering grass,
and they nibble the bark
from the trees that they pass.

Splendid brown coats under
winter-white skies
are a peaceful sight
as the sun starts to rise.

Then the crack of a twig
and the snap of a stick
send them scattering out,
running quickety-quick!

Startled, the elegant animals race,
darting this way and that and all over the place.

And then up ahead strides a wondrous beast, calling,
"Come, settle down, and continue your feast."

The buck struts and swaggers
and tosses his head,
with a crown not of gold
but of antlers instead.

Watching him closely,
the others draw near
and they all sing together,
The Song of the Deer.

"We are the keepers.
We watch and we know

every branch on each tree,
every root down below.

We smell every scene
and we hear every sound,
from the birdsong above
to the life underground.

The forest shelters us.
It keeps us from harm,
for a wood full of life
is a world full of calm.

This forest is ours
and together we're strong.
In the meadows we roam,
in the woods we belong!"

Their song has now ended
and Buck walks away.
Perhaps their paths
will cross again one fine day.

All about WHITE-TAILED DEER

White-tailed deer are HERBIVORES (plant eaters) that lead shy, quiet lives in woods and meadows. Able to run at speeds up to thirty miles per hour and leap ten feet in the air, they are well equipped to escape predators.

Female deer are called DOES.

Male deer are called BUCKS. Bucks herd separately from does and fawns.

Baby deer are called FAWNS. They are born in the spring with white spots that fade by late summer.

White-tailed deer are largely crepuscular, which means they are most active at dawn and dusk.

Bucks have magnificent, multi-pointed antlers made of bone. They shed and grow a new pair every year!

The forest is filled
with an evening glow

as the **DEER** start to gallop . . .
Now where will they go?

The FLIGHT of BLACKBIRDS

Up in the branches and high overhead,
there's a cluster of eggs in a nest like a bed.

Safe in the space
under Mama Bird's chest,
every powder-blue egg
has its place in the nest.

One starts to quiver,
another one shakes.
There's a pop and a crack
as another one breaks!

With a push and a shove,
a tiny beak pokes through.

"Hello, Baby Bird One! Hello, Baby Bird Two!"

"Cheep, cheep!" cries a third
as they hatch from their eggs.
Before long they can stand
up on baby bird legs.

"Morning!" sings Mama Bird,
"Open your eyes!
I will fetch you some worms,"
and with that . . . off she flies.

Hungry and thirsty,
together they squeak
with a twitter and chatter
from each baby beak.

"Feed us, oh feed us!"
the baby birds cry.
*"For we need to grow feathers
in order to fly!"*

*"We need to grow MIGHTY!
We need to grow WINGS!
We need to grow FLIGHTY!"*
the third baby sings.

Mama Bird carries
her worms to the nest.

The baby birds gobble,
then afterward, rest!

At night, Mama snuggles
her baby birds three,
and they sleep safe and warm
in their nest in the tree.

Each day they grow with their eyes on the sky,
until each one is feathered and ready to fly!

Then the little birds practice
by flapping their wings,
and they

JUMP!

from

the

nest

on invisible strings.

Slowly at first, and then higher they rise,

singing, *"Look at us fly!"* as they head for the skies.

Many months later . . .

and now they are strong
as they murmur and glide
like the notes of a song.

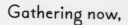

Gathering now,

like a cloud in the sky,

they flow just as fast

as a river goes by!

Together they fly

over meadow and sea.

Oh, a bird in the air

is the best thing to be!

All about
BLACKBIRDS

In winter, large flocks of blackbirds gather together.

They ripple and flow across the sky in flocks called RIVERS or CLOUDS.

Sometimes, they join starlings in acrobatic displays called MURMURATIONS.

Why do they do it? Well, there's safety in numbers! Large flocks make it harder for predators to single out one bird.

They also keep warmer when together and exchange important information. In other words, this gathering is the perfect way to catch up on the latest gossip!

Where will they go
in their flowing display?

Let's follow the **BLACKBIRDS**
up, up, and away!

The MAGICAL METAMORPHOSIS of FROGS

Down in the pond, there are thousands of dots . . .
They are bubble-tea tiny with little black spots!

They float on the surface
like quivering blobs
in a jellified jumble
of thing-a-ma-bobs.

Once they are ready, they pop through the spawn,
and ta-da! All the miniature tadpoles are born!

These tiny commas—
no bigger than seeds—
wiggle each teeny tail
and relax by the reeds.

Squiggles of ink
in a weedy green pond,
each with two beady eyes
on the forest beyond.

They grow and they grow,
through the water they sail.
Little quivering notes
flicking each mini tail.

"This is the life!" all the tadpoles agree.
"Yes, a pond in the woods is the best place to be!"

"The algae is tasty,"
says one with a sigh,
"but I'd rather munch on
a succulent fly . . ."

The lily pads twitch–there is movement beneath.
All the tadpoles are growing some miniature . . . teeth!

"We've come a long way
from our jellified eggs!"

say the tadpoles, admiring
their newly grown legs.

"Look at us kicking!"
the tiny tads roar.
"Two legs are fantastic
but how about . . . four!"

Plump froggy bodies
and fine-flippered feet . . .
now the tad transformation
is almost complete!

"Imagine," says one,
"what awaits far beyond:
all the pea-soupy gloop
of this watery pond!"

Daytime brings sunshine
and sparkling showers,
a pond filled with water
and a wood full of flowers.

"Pond life is lovely,"
the froglets declare,
*"but we want an adventure
and maybe fresh air!"*

"Hey," says another,
"let's jump to dry ground!"
Then it hops and it lands without
making a sound.

More froglets follow
and bounce over logs.
Then their tails disappear
as they turn into frogs!

Dry land and water!
The frogs all agree
that a pond in the woods
is the best place to be.

All about FROG METAMORPHOSIS

A frog's life cycle has many stages. During each stage, the frog changes and grows, so that over the course of its life it goes through an amazing transformation. This process is called METAMORPHOSIS.

1. A frog begins life in a pond as a tiny EGG in a jumble of eggs called FROGSPAWN.

2. When the eggs hatch, tiny TADPOLES emerge with long tails for swimming.

During a frog's METAMORPHOSIS, an egg will hatch into a TADPOLE, which will then develop back legs first, then front legs, and keeps growing and changing until it becomes a fully grown adult frog! The whole process takes about sixteen weeks, from the start as a FROGSPAWN to a grown FROG.

3. After several weeks, the tadpole grows LEGS!

4. With four legs, the tadpole is now a tiny frog: a FROGLET.

5. The long tail shrinks and the tadpole starts to grow lungs for breathing air.

6. Once the tail disappears and its lungs are fully grown, the froglet is a FROG!

And there goes a **FROG,**
setting off from the pond.

But what will he meet
in the forest beyond?

The HIDDEN GREAT HORNED OWL

Look in the nook of that gnarly old tree-
are there animals hiding inside, can you see?

Mottled brown markings
fade into the bark
as they silently watch
the woods in the dark . . .

These owls are clever,
they're ever so wise,
wearing camouflage feathers:
the perfect disguise!

A flutter of yellow or flicker of beak—
explore every cranny to find what you seek!

"The cool of a hollow,
the shade of a tree,
in a thicket or snag
are the places we'll be!"

And there they will rest
for the day is for sleep,
only waking again
when the dusk starts to creep . . .

Then ever so softly one calls, "Hoo-hoo-hooo . . .
Shall I hunt for a meal? Yes, that's what I'll do!"

And he swoops from his roost
over meadow and field
using powerful wings
like a feathery shield.

*"I rest every day in the nook of a tree,
but up high in the sky is the place I am free!"*

Watching and listening,
he soars through the night—
an invisible glider,
a master of flight . . .

With claws at the ready
and two steady eyes
all the better for spotting,
he plots his . . . *surprise!*

A shadow falls over
the meadow below,

and the mice start to scatter—
oh where will they go?

The mice are too quick
and they scuttle away,

so the owl must keep flying
to find some more prey.

Owl searches around,
for he's hoping to see
if his mate is awake
in the nook of the tree . . .

She is! And, *"Good morning!"*
"Good morning!" he sings
as he lands by her side
on inaudible wings.

She hoots to him softly,
*"My love, close your eyes.
Let us rest until dusk
comes again to the skies . . ."*

All about CAMOUFLAGE

Horned owls are famous for their fantastic CAMOUFLAGE,
which makes them great hunters.

Their BRIGHT YELLOW EYES are the biggest of any owl species. If the horned owl were as big as a human its eyes would be the size of oranges!

They have SUPERB LOW-LIGHT AND NIGHT VISION, doing most of their HUNTING at dusk or before dawn. Mice are one of their favorite foods.

Horned owls don't actually have horns. Instead, they have tufts of feathers on their heads called PLUMICORNS. These tufts look like twigs and help horned owls blend into their environments.

OWL EYES CAN'T MOVE but their flexible necks can turn 270 DEGREES. So it really does look like they have eyes in the back of their heads!

They are MONOGAMOUS, meaning they mate for life and care for their OWLETS together. Owl couples also sing a lovely hoo-hoo-hooing song.

The **OWLS** slip away,
singing lullaby hoots . . .

Shall we see where they fly
on their nightly pursuits?

The STAG BEETLE'S SEVEN-YEAR FEAST

Into the forest
and farther around,
a little grub lives
in a log on the ground.

The log was a tree
that had fallen and died.
So the wood in the log
is quite rotten inside.

It's deliciously rotten
and ready to munch,
so the little grub eats it
for breakfast and lunch.

The wood is so yummy,
and the little grub knows
that the more that it gobbles,
the more it will grow.

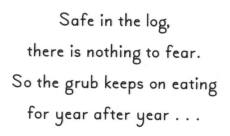

Safe in the log,
there is nothing to fear.
So the grub keeps on eating
for year after year . . .

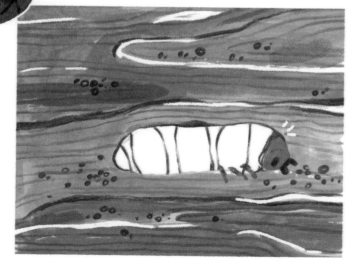

Through the sun and the rain, in the warm and the cold,
hungry little Grub eats till it's seven years old!

With a diet like this, it's not a surprise
that Grub has grown bigger and bigger in size.

"I'm full," says Grub, "I am perfectly stout.
I believe I am ready to munch my way out..."

Once on the surface,
Grub looks around—
then it digs in the earth
for a bed underground . . .

There it changes from a grub
to a beetle with shell,
and in several weeks
grows some antlers as well!

The following spring, in a powerful gust,

a fierce-looking creature appears from the dust!

By summer the creature
is handsome and bright—
he's a stag beetle warrior:
ready to fight!

Stag Beetle looks mighty –
he certainly should –
because most of his life
has been spent eating wood!

But marvelous mouthparts make walking slow.
So he opens his wings, crying, *"Come on, let's go!"*

"*For this is the end of my journey,*" says he, "*after such a long time as a grub in a tree.*

But now I must hurry, for I have a date with a beautiful beetle and cannot be late."

With a rumbling hum and a shimmering sheen, Stag Beetle takes off like a flying machine.

He wobbles a bit as he hovers in flight. Then he zips on his way as day turns to night!

All about the STAG BEETLE'S LIFE CYCLE

With their huge, antler-like MANDIBLES (mouthparts), male stag beetles are one of the world's largest beetles. Incredibly, they spend most of their life underground as larvae, only emerging for a few weeks to find a mate and reproduce.

1. The beetle starts life as an EGG.

2. The egg hatches into a GRUB. It spends five to seven years eating ROTTING WOOD.

6. The BEETLE lives a FEW MONTHS at most.

When male stag beetles fly, they seem to defy gravity! Their wings make a deep, humming sound and they look like miniature helicopters. These digesting eco superheroes quietly recycle waste with every bite, spending nearly all their life eating rotting wood!

5. The following spring, the ADULT STAG BEETLE emerges!

3. The GRUB emerges from wood, then digs UNDERGROUND and becomes a PUPA.

4. It takes around SIX WEEKS to transform into an adult beetle.

The march of the **BEETLE**
is steady and strong.

He needs to keep moving—
can we come along?

The DANCE of the HONEYBEE

Wide meadow, wild meadow, bathing in sun,
like a city of grass where the meadow mice run.

Butterflies flutter
all over the place,
while the flowers explode
into petals of lace.

Cornflowers burst
in a banquet of blooms,
growing tall in the field
where a honeybee zooms.

The honeybee pauses
and smells the cool air.
She senses the sweetness
that drifts everywhere.

"Our pollen is precious," the flowers all say.

*"Please scatter and spread it,
for this is the way!"*

Bee collects pollen,
putting all she can hold
in her two little sacks,
each one brimming with gold.

From flower to flower,
she gathers with skill.
Her bags are so heavy,
they're starting to spill!

The daisies are beaming–
they turn to the sun
while the honeybee gathers
until she is done.

"As thanks, we give you
the sweetest reward—
this sugary nectar to
add to your hoard!"

The honeybee dips with a satisfied hum
and sucks up the liquid to store in her tum.

Then quickly she hurries
straight back to the hive.
So giddy with nectar,
she dances a jive!

"Honeybee, honeybee,
why are you late?"
Bee buzzes around
in a smooth figure eight.

"Honeybee, honeybee,
what have you seen?"
"I saw a great meadow
with food for the queen!"

"Honeybee, honeybee,
tell us, from where?"
"Around by the daisies,
away over there!"

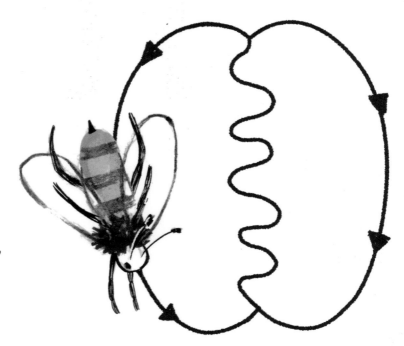

And back by the hive
in a mystical trance,
she wiggles and waggles
the honeybee dance!

The daisies are swaying,
the meadow is warm,
and high in the sunshine
the honeybees swarm.

The pollen they gather,
the nectar they hold,
are richer than riches,
more precious than gold.

An everyday miracle
bursting with powers—
the wonder of bees
in a meadow of flowers!

All about BEES and POLLINATION

POLLINATION is the journey that flowering plants take to reproduce. It happens when pollen is moved from one flower to another and it allows the plant to make seeds that will grow into new plants. Many plants rely on POLLINATORS to move the pollen from flower to flower. Bees are pollinators, so they are an essential part of this process.

1. A flower's male parts make a powdery substance called POLLEN.

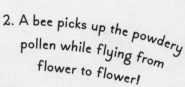

2. A bee picks up the powdery pollen while flying from flower to flower!

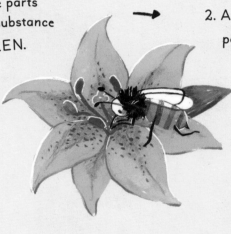

3. POLLINATION happens when the bee drops pollen on another flower. The flower will go on to make seeds.

7. The honeybee WAGGLE DANCE is a figure-eight boogie that tells other bees the exact location of a food supply. (It's basically GPS for bees!)

All sorts of plants rely on bees to pollinate them, and bees need plants to live and make honey. A third of our food is thanks to bees. We simply can't exist without them!

6. As a reward for the bees' hard work, flowers give them a sugary liquid called NECTAR. And it's nectar that bees turn into their most famous product: glorious, golden honey!

5. Bees carry the pollen they collect in mini saddlebags on their legs.

4. The bees also gather the pollen to take back to feed their family.

While **HONEYBEES**
wiggle and waggle at home,

away from the **MEADOW,**
there's farther to roam . . .

The LiTTLE RaBBiT and the GREEN MaCHiNE

Down in the meadow, not making a sound,
a rabbit is snuggled asleep on the ground.

The meadow is peaceful,
wide open and sunny.
The field full of grasses
just right for a bunny!

She nibbles the flowers
and gobbles the plants,
skipping this way and that
in a bouncy spring dance.

But one day she wonders,
Perhaps there is more . . .
And she leaps from the
meadow and goes to explore.

It doesn't take long
till she hoppity-hops
to a thicket of trees,
where she finally stops.

The little gray rabbit hops into the glade,
where she sits by a sapling, then flops in its shade!

She looks from the ground
to the branches up high
and she sees where the tips
of the trees touch the sky.

She thinks to herself, *This is wonderfully green.*
It's the loveliest forest I ever have seen!

This wood full of wonder was waiting for me.
There is nowhere on earth that I'd much rather be!

She waits for a while and stares up at the sky,
but she doesn't ask, "*How?*" And she doesn't ask, "*Why?*"

Because tiny to mighty,
each living thing knows
there's magic in greenness—
and here's how it goes . . .

The chlorophyll found
in a plant that is green
helps it become
a sunshine machine!

Each leaf on a tree
and every grass blade
turns light into energy,
perfectly made!

See, all of these plants
make their food from the sun.
And they even give oxygen
after they're done!

And oxygen gas is a fine thing indeed—
in the air we breathe in, it's the thing that we need.

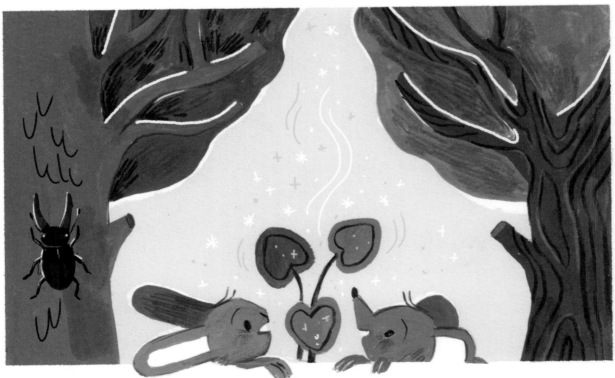

But carbon dioxide—the waste gas we give—
is the gas that the trees and all plants need to live!

The rabbit sits down
on a comfortable root
and she gobbles some grass,
then she nibbles a shoot.

Because tiny to mighty,
each living thing knows:
There's magic in greenness,
that's just how it goes.

All about PHOTOSYNTHESIS

PHOTOSYNTHESIS is the process by which green plants use sunlight to make their own food. Without photosynthesis, there would be no green plants—and without green plants, there would be no animals!

For photosynthesis, plants need SUNLIGHT, CHLOROPHYLL, and CARBON DIOXIDE. Plants get carbon dioxide from the air, and water from the soil.

They use the ENERGY in sunlight and water to change carbon dioxide into SUGARS. The waste they make is oxygen, the gas that animals (including humans) need to breathe!

So plants really are BIG, GREEN SUNSHINE MACHINES!

The **RABBIT** explores
with a hop and a skip.

Shall we see who she meets
on her very next trip?

The MOTH and the MOOn

Tiger moth, tiger moth,
fiery bright,
she rests in the day
and she flies through the night . . .

As soon as the moon
rises over the sky,
the tiger moth wakes,
for she needs it to fly.

By moonlight she figures the right way to go,
as she flies in the light of its ivory glow.

Tracing the path from her heavenly map,
she follows a line with each fluttering flap . . .

She stops for a moment
to stare up at the moon,
and she whispers a wish
that her love will come soon.

"Oh Moon, lovely Moon,
ever shining above.
I'm a moth on a mission—
I'm looking for love!

But how will I do it?
I'm silent and small.
With no voice nor a roar,
he won't hear me at all!"

The moon gazes down
on the moth far below
and she says with a smile,
"There are some things I know . . .

Stop looking for love
and your love will find you—
just stay on your journey
and make it come true!"

"The music of silence
is sometimes the best.
You must let Mother Nature
take care of the rest!"

The moon spreads her glow,
and the moth seems to sail
as she launches behind her
a sweet-smelling trail . . .

In an instant, straight out of the indigo black,

there's a tumble of followers right on her track . . .

This tiger-like moth, with a fire in her wings,
leaves a wonderful scent. Can you see what it brings?

A crowd draws near as the sweet smell diffuses.
Each moth wants to be the one that she chooses!

Too many to choose from,
too many to meet!
The moth is delighted,
her journey complete.

"Goodnight, little moth.
All your worries are gone!"
And the tiger moth rests
knowing life will go on . . .

All about MOTHS

Moths can fly in straight lines by using a fixed angle to the Moon.
This skill is called TRANSVERSE ORIENTATION and
it's a sort of moth navigational system!

The moth in the story is a
striking TIGER MOTH.

There are more than 250 species
of tiger moths in North America.
They are known for having
wings with bold patterns
and bright colors.

Tiger moths are nocturnal
(more active at night) so
they must find mates in the
darkness. They do this by
releasing a powerful pheromone
(that's a fancy word for scent).
Male moths find it irresistible.
As soon as they catch a
whiff, they come flocking.

Tiger moths are clever—they can
confuse bats (their main predator) by
making sonar clicks (or "sound pulses")
just like the bats make.

Tiger moth caterpillars are known as "woolly bears"
because that's what they look like. Adorable!

As the silvery moon lights the dark sleepy wood,
each 5-minute story will do what it should!

Each creature,
each tree,
every lovely surprise.
What a world full of wonder
in front of our eyes!

FURTHER READING

Life Cycles: Everything from Start to Finish by DK Publishing and illustrated by Sam Falconer

The Mushroom Fan Club by Elise Gravel

Nature All Around series by Pamela Hickman and illustrated by Carolyn Gavin

Slow Down: 50 Mindful Moments in Nature by Rachel Williams and illustrated by Freya Hartas

The Wonders of Nature by Ben Hoare and illustrated by Angela Rizza and Daniel Long

For Michael –G.D.

The illustrations in this book were created using gouache, colored pencil, and digital media.
Set in Bakerie, Claytonia, Pistachio, and Quicksand.

Library of Congress Control Number 2022944940
ISBN 978-1-4197-6775-3

Text © 2022 Gabby Dawnay
Illustrations © 2022 Mona K
Cover © 2022 Magic Cat
Book design by Nicola Price and Maisy Ruffels

Printed and bound in China
10 9 8 7 6 5

Abrams Books are available at special discounts when purchased in quantity for premiums and promotions as well as fundraising or educational use. Special editions can also be created to specification. For details, contact specialsales@abramsbooks.com or the address below.

MIX
Paper | Supporting responsible forestry
FSC® C104723
www.fsc.org

ABRAMS The Art of Books
195 Broadway, New York, NY 10007
abramsbooks.com